B&B Know-How

B&B Know-How

How to Make Money From Your Spare Room

Amy Willcock

EBURY
PRESS

First published in Great Britain in 2005

First published by Ebury Publishing
Random House, 20 Vauxhall Bridge Road, London SW1V 2SA

Random House Australia (Pty) Limited
20 Alfred Street, Milsons Point, Sydney, New South Wales 2061, Australia

Random House New Zealand Limited
18 Poland Road, Glenfield, Auckland 10, New Zealand

Random House South Africa (Pty) Limited
Endulini, 5A Jubilee Road, Parktown 2193, South Africa

The Random House Group Limited Reg. No. 954009

www.randomhouse.co.uk

A CIP catalogue record for this book is available from the British Library.

ISBN 0091900751

Editor: Gillian Haslam
Designer: Nicky Barneby
Illustrations: Lizzie Collcutt

Printed and bound in Great Britain by
Mackays of Chatham plc, Chatham, Kent

About the author

In 1980, Amy Willcock moved from the USA to the UK
with her parents to enter the world of B&B. The project that
started as a retirement amusement for her parents grew
into a thriving business of three B&Bs and a hotel. When
Amy married hotelier Jeremy Willcock she stayed in the
business. Amy runs lifestyle and Aga workshops, has a
regular column in *The Shooting Gazette*, and writes for
several magazines, including *Homes and Gardens*,
Waitrose Food Illustrated and *Sainsbury's Magazine*. She
is the author of four best-selling books: *Aga Cooking*,
Amy Willcock's Aga Baking, *Amy Willcock's Aga Know-How*
and *Amy Willcock's Aga Seasons*. She can be contacted at
www.amywillcock.co.uk

Contents

'B&B is the best fun – I love it!'

Chef and cookery writer Orlando Murrin, editorial director of *BBC Good Food* and *Olive* magazines, and author of three bestselling cookery books. See page 121 for details of his B&B in France.

Introduction

THE SECRET OF running a successful Bed & Breakfast is down to three things: charm, location and a fantastic breakfast.

My aim with this book is to give you all the information you need to run a B&B to the highest level. The book is full of information, advice, tips and, of course, cooking instructions for the perfect breakfast.

The B&B market is often an 'Aga market' and my expertise in Aga cooking has led to my receiving many requests from B&B owners about catering for their guests. There is a natural crossover from my Aga cookbook readers, and escaping to the country is booming in the 30–40-year age group. It is amazing that for the price of a couple of West End cinema tickets and a bag of popcorn, you can get accommodation of real quality up and down the country.

When my family first moved to the UK from the US, my parents wanted to get out of the rat race and live a better, less pressured life. So they embarked on what was to become an even busier, more hectic life, but one full of fun, friendships and cash! Our first B&B had six letting rooms and I used to help cook and serve breakfast when home from school. What set us apart from any other B&B was my parents' enthusiasm and good old-fashioned 'can do' spirit – I guess we were pioneers in our own way. My father is the perfect host and my mother has the business brains.

Any B&B owner will tell you that the overwhelming requirements for running a really good B&B are a love of people and a clean house. It seems that very successful B&B owners can have the tiniest rooms with very basic WC facilities and can still be full all year round due entirely to the fact that they are such charming hosts!

The reason people choose to stay at a B&B is that they like the personal touches and the less formal atmosphere they find there. The hosts and houses tend to be full of interesting characteristics and they offer great value for money. Usually the relaxed, informal and friendly way in which they are run suits host and guest alike. Quite often beautiful country B&Bs will have added bonuses such as fantastic gardens, or serve foods like home-made jam and eggs from the family chickens. In cities some B&Bs add a real sense of home to a guest's stay that a hotel just can't compete with, especially if they find themselves working away from home Monday to Friday.

I want to equip you with everything you need to know about running a B&B at the top end of the market. You can adjust my guidelines to suit your property or way of life, but I do hope you will have fun and find it a happy and fun way to make money from your spare rooms!

Frequently Asked Questions

What you will need to run a B+B

Different types of accommodation

Provisions for guests

Guidebooks and inspections

Maintaining contacts

B+B Etiquette

1

If you can't cook anything else you must know how to boil an egg!

Q Do I need a big house to run a B&B?

A No. Even if you only have a two-bedroomed house – one
for you and one for your guests – you can do B&B
successfully. If it is possible, make your letting bedroom
the one with ensuite facilities.

Q Do I have to be a good cook to run a B&B?

A No, but the skill you must perfect is making a good
breakfast. Even if you can't cook anything else, you must
know how to boil an egg! Breakfast is the last memory
guests have of their stay, so you want to make sure
they go away thinking that they will come back or, even
better, recommend you to their friends. Contact me at
www.amywillcock.co.uk for information about my
B&B Know-How workshops.

Q Do I need any experience?

A No, you can start straight away. Most people have friends to stay occasionally and will already have an idea of how they like to be treated when staying away from home. Follow the guidelines in this book and you will be fine. The biggest decision about starting a B&B is being honest with yourself and deciding whether you are the sort of person who will be good with people and cope with having strangers in the house.

Q **What is the difference between an inn, guesthouse, boarding house, hotel and B&B?**

A An inn is a public house providing accommodation and refreshments for travellers.

A guesthouse is a house where strangers, especially holidaymakers, are accommodated. Usually lower end of the market.

A boarding house is a house offering board and lodging for a weekly rate. Usually lower end of the market.

A hotel is an establishment of comfortable or luxurious levels of fittings and design where paying visitors are provided with accommodation, meals and other services, ranging from spas to business centres.

A B&B provides warm and friendly overnight accommodation and breakfast in a homely atmosphere.

Q What time do guests arrive and depart?

A Check-in is usually from tea-time, which means any time from 4 p.m. to early evening. Guests will usually let you know if they are going to be late but you can ask what time they intend to arrive when they make the booking.

Check-out is usually between 11 a.m. and 12 p.m. Make this clear either in the bedroom literature or when they are checking in. Sometimes guests will want to leave their luggage for collection later in the day.

Q Do I have to provide dinner?

A No, B&B is exactly that. However, some B&Bs are located in the middle of nowhere and like to offer dinner at a set price. If you are an enthusiastic cook, then this provides a wonderful showcase for all your recipes. I suggest offering a set 3-course dinner with coffee. Selling alcohol will mean a licence and that may be a step too far, so you could tell your guests to bring their own wine for dinner.

Wolsey Lodges (see page 125) is an organisation B&Bs can belong to. It's a great set-up that does require the hosts to cook dinner. They are fun places to stay and I highly recommend a trip to one if you are considering serving dinner to see how it's done.

Some B&Bs offer afternoon tea and packed picnic lunches, so for the person who really is a frustrated chef at heart go for gold and cook away! Do remember that the cooking will take a lot of time in preparation, serving and washing up.

Q Which is the best guide for me to be in?

A This is where you will need to do some research. Start by asking yourself some basic questions such as: am I in a rural area and will therefore have a more touristy type of customer, or am I in the town or city and will attract a business customer? When doing your research, look for the type of customer the guide is attracting and go from there. Ask the guides for figures of how many bed nights you can expect from them and contact the other B&Bs in the guide to find out how satisfied they are with the business they get from the guide.

Q What do I have to do to reach a star rating in the guide books?

A Each organisation has its own set of standards and criteria to fulfil. You will need to contact whichever organisation you would like to belong to and ask for a copy of their guidelines. If the guidelines are achievable in your B&B, fill in the registration form and wait for an inspection which you may or may not know about until it is all over.

Q Do you know beforehand that an inspector is coming round? What do you do if their comments are negative?

A You will usually be notified beforehand with a first inspection, but each organisation is different and some are covert. The AA offers a service whereby you pay to be inspected to help you achieve your potential. This is arranged by you, then an inspection takes place and you are given a full report. If the comments are negative, only you will be able to assess whether they are correct observations or not. Sometimes it is just not possible to fulfil all the criteria they ask for, perhaps because a room is physically the wrong size, or you will never meet a certain aspect of the inspection because you decide that isn't how you want to run your B&B. On the other hand, if the comment was that the housekeeping was not up to standard, you will have to look at your standards and put it right, or if it was that the breakfast was badly cooked you may have to take yourself off to a cookery school!

Q **Is it worth sending out follow-up material to guests after they've stayed? Perhaps informing them of local events, and just reminding them of my existence, or keeping a database of guests' addresses to send out Christmas cards or updates on the B&B?**

A A database is extremely useful and I strongly recommend that you keep one. A really useful way of getting to your customers is through e-mail. Set up a newsletter to be sent at certain times of the year with all the relevant events, etc. You can do this by post but you may find it expensive if your database is very large. Use your website (see page 101) and direct all your clients to it for information. Website management is crucial for this and keeping it up to date is paramount.

Q **What should I expect from my guests and what should I do if they ask me about tipping?**

A B&B can be a social minefield – if guests don't understand the etiquette, things can get a little awkward.

Guests should behave as if in an hotel. They have paid for the room so don't expect them to have made the bed. They should be aware of other guests and try not to come in late and make lots of noise or be hideously untidy in the room.

If you decide to provide an evening meal, in some houses guests dine with the family, while other houses provide a separate dining room. Make it clear how you expect the guest to dress for dinner and what the dress code is for breakfast if you think the guest needs guidance.

Tipping is an art form so work out what your tipping policy is. Some B&Bs find the easiest solution is to leave a tip box in the hall.

The perfect guest arrives at the B&B between 5 and 6 p.m., so make this clear when the booking is made. Earlier or later times can be made by prior arrangement.

Getting Started

Are you ready to take the plunge?
Location, location, location

If you like having people around you,
you'll make a good host.

BEFORE EMBARKING ON your B&B adventure, you must ask yourself three fundamental questions:

- Will I make a good host?
- Am I a 'people person'?
- Will my family help me or hinder me?

If you are outgoing, a good conversationalist and like having people around you, then the answer is yes: you will make a good host. If, however, you are a shy, retiring person who doesn't like too many disruptions or strangers in the house, then don't go any further.

Are You Ready to Take the Plunge?

If you feel that members of your household or family
will oppose the idea, you need to think very carefully.
Concessions will have to be made and there are times
when your house is not your own. Talk it through with family
members and chat to other B&B owners; go and stay at a
B&B to show your family how it works and what will be
expected. Teenagers can earn pocket money from helping
out and they can be invaluable for taking bookings,
housekeeping and serving breakfast.

Once you have established that you are the right
person/family to run a B&B, the world is your oyster. All that
you have to do now is decide how you want to run it – will it
be the type of B&B that has lots of added extras or will you
run it on a fairly basic level? People choose to stay at B&Bs
because they like the home-from-home atmosphere that a
B&B has, in contrast to an impersonal chain hotel.

There is a brilliant guide called *The Pink Booklet* published by Visit Britain – it is a practical guide to legislation for accommodation providers and I strongly recommend you buy it (see page 125).

Location, Location, Location

If you are planning to open a B&B, you can either do it from the house you currently live in or, if you are thinking of running it as a full-time business, acquire a property for that purpose. If you are doing it from home as a way of making money from the spare room, location, while important, is not as vital as it would be if you wanted to run it as a full-time business.

There are two schools of thought on location: one is that if you go where others are it must be a good location; and the other is that if you go where others are not, you can be the market leader – so it is a decision that you need to make. I would always go for a good area and compromise on the house rather than a great house in a bad area. I would definitely buy the house of my dreams and consider running a B&B to make up the mortgage if it came to the crunch.

For a town B&B, the best location is probably in the town centre or on a main road leading into town. Victorian townhouses lend themselves well for B&B as the rooms are spacious and ensuite bathrooms can be added easily.

In the country you will want a house with good access to a pub or restaurant serving great food and country pursuits such as walks and historical sites. Look for country houses with outhouses that can be converted for B&B or houses that can easily separate into two areas – family area and letting rooms.

The size of the property doesn't really matter as long as you can give a customer a bedroom and bathroom of their own and somewhere to serve breakfast. I know of a tiny lodge next to a castle that does B&B. All they have are two bedrooms – one for the owners and one (ensuite) to let, which proves you don't have to have a huge house.

Whatever the location, the main requirement is that the bedrooms must be either ensuite or with their own bathroom – no one will share a bathroom in the 21st century.

Keeping it Legal

Planning permission
Fire safety
Environmental health office
Insurance cover
B+B overseas

Do your homework, and keep up to date with rules and regulations.

BEFORE YOU OPEN your B&B, contact your local council planning department, environmental health office and fire authority to find out the precise requirements and regulations for running a B&B in your area. In this book I give general advice, but as regulations vary from one council to another and are frequently updated, it is essential to contact your own council. Before you go off looking at property for the purpose of establishing a B&B, it will be helpful to know what you need to look out for in terms of the local council's specifications.

Planning Permission

The local council planning departments work on a 'matter of fact and degree' policy when it comes to B&Bs. There isn't a specific point at which planning kicks in. They are concerned with the 'proportion and frequency of the property', which means how much of the property is being used for B&B and how often. They are looking for any alterations to the character of the property when changing from a house to a business. Signage is an area that you may also need to discuss with them (see page 36). Another point to consider is that if the property is in an area of out-standing natural beauty or in a conservation area, you may have to consult with the relevant committees.

Fire Safety

The whole point of fire safety is prevention. The Fire Authority is brilliant at giving goodwill advice about fire safety. I take the view that if you are going to have people in your house, then you will want to keep them as safe as your own family.

It is imperative to install smoke detectors. If you have a large house, you can link them together and run them off the mains – this saves a huge amount of bother when it comes to changing batteries, as one of the most common problems with smoke detectors is that people just turn them off when the battery runs out because the beep is so annoying. They then forget to replace the battery, rendering them completely useless.

You should also install a fire blanket in the kitchen as well as a dry powder fire extinguisher. Make sure you know how to use them.

As many household fires are caused by faulty wiring, do get an electrician to check your electrics.

The current code of practice states that:

'A fire certificate will not be required unless either sleeping accommodation is for more than six persons whether they are staff or guests, or some of the sleeping accommodation is above the first floor level, or some of the sleeping accommodation is below the ground floor level.'

[Taken from Guide to Fire Precautions in premises used as hotels and boarding houses which require a fire certificate, published by the Home Office, correct at time of going to press.]

There is a lack of consistency throughout the country and across different tourism and marketing bodies in general for establishments providing accommodation, so a new Order is coming into practice to close the gap. The Fire Precaution Act 1971 will be replaced by the Regulatory Reform Order in late 2004.

In each bedroom you should also clearly display a plan of how to get out of the house in the event of an emergency.

Environmental Health Office

You will need to register with your local environmental health office and attend a basic food hygiene course. Contact your local council EHO for more advice. They can usually provide government advice on starting up a small business, covering subjects such as food, health and safety which you need to understand before you start your B&B. Go to their website for more details: http://www.hse.gov.uk/startup/index.htm

Overleaf is an extract from my local EHO website (www.iwight.com/living_here/environment/environmental_health).

What is registration?

1. Registration of premises used for a food business (including market stalls, delivery vehicles and other moveable structures) is required by law. Registration will allow local authorities to keep an up-to-date list of all those premises in their area so they can visit them when they need to. The frequency of the visits will depend on the type of business.

Who needs to register?

2. If you run a food business for more than 5 days in any 5 consecutive weeks, you must tell (or arrange for someone else to tell) the local authority about any premises you use for storing, selling, distributing or preparing food. Food premises include restaurants, hotels, cafes, shops, supermarkets, staff canteens, kitchens in offices, warehouses, guest houses, delivery vehicles, buffet cars on trains, market and other stalls, hot-dog and ice-cream vans, etc.

3. If you use vehicles for your food business in connection with permanent premises such as a shop or warehouse, you only need to tell the local authority how many vehicles you have. You do not need to register each vehicle separately. If you have one or more vehicles but no permanent premises, you must tell the authority where they are normally kept.

4. Anyone starting a new food business must register with the local authority at least 28 days before doing so.

5. The majority of premises will have to be registered. However, certain premises are exempt from registration, e.g. some that are already registered for food law purposes, certain agricultural premises, motor cars, tents and marquees (but not stalls), some domestic premises and some village halls. You should contact your local authority if you think you might be exempt.

How do I register?

6. By filling in the relevant form. Registration cannot be refused and there is no charge. The registration form must be sent to your local authority. The address can be found in the telephone directory. If the form is sent to the wrong address your application will not take effect until it is received at the proper place. If you use premises in more than one local authority area, you must register with each authority separately.

7. You must tick all the boxes that apply to your business, answer all the questions and give all the information requested. Seasonal businesses operating for a certain period each year should give the dates between which they will be open in answer. If you have any questions your local authority will help you. It is an offence to give information that you know is false.

What happens to the information given on the form?

8. The local authority will enter the details on its Register. A register of addresses and the type of business carried on at each will be open to inspection by the general public. Records of the other information provided will not be publicly available.

Changes

9. Once you have registered with the Local Authority you only need notify them of a change of proprietor, if the nature of the business changes, or if there is a change of the address at which moveable premises are kept. The new proprietor will have to complete an application form.

If the local authority wishes to change the entry in the Register because of information that it receives from someone else, you will be given 28 days' notice and an opportunity to comment on the proposed change. These notes are provided for information only and should not be regarded as a complete statement of the law.

Insurance Cover

This section will make you aware of your responsibilities as a B&B provider. Once you open your doors to the public you come under the Occupiers' Liability Acts 1957 and 1984. This means that the person who is in charge of the premises is liable for the physical safety of everyone (children as well as adults) who comes onto their premises – this includes stepping onto their property whether you make it inside the door or not! Note: In some incidents this applies to trespassers.

You must practise due care and diligence. So be aware of things like faulty handrails or uneven steps or paths, make sure cables are not posing a risk to anyone, lay out emergency procedures clearly and precisely, making sure the guests are acquainted with them, and many more ...

If you employ even just one member of staff, all this applies to them too. The owner of the premises can be held responsible for any accidents caused as a result of negligence due to staff or other guests. All areas that are out of bounds to guests should be clearly marked, but staff will still be affected.

It doesn't matter how many disclaimer notices you put up, you will still be liable for death or injuries resulting from negligence, so my advice is to take out proper and adequate insurance cover and get informed!

Take out public liability insurance. Your normal household insurance policy will probably not include this and some insurers provide all-inclusive policies for people who do B&B. The sort of package you will want is:

- Public liability insurance
- Employers' liability insurance*
- Property and contents insurance

* For information on all Health and Safety aspects in the workplace and employers' liability, contact: Employers' Liability (compulsory insurance) Act 1969 Health and Safety Executive. Information line 08701 545500, website www.hse.gov.uk

You cannot discriminate between people – colour, creed, disability, sex and age don't come into the equation when you employ someone.

B&B Overseas

If you are thinking of opening up a B&B abroad, it is best to contact the embassy for that country to find out details regarding legislation. A friend of mine has opened a B&B in France and is loving every minute of it but there is a very different legislation system, so do your homework and learn the language.

Creating A Welcome

You never get a second chance to make a good first impression.

I DON'T KNOW who said this but it is so true and applies to everything in life, particularly a B&B: 'You never get a second chance to make a good first impression'. The front of your house, the sign, the drive, the path, the garden and the front door all contribute to this first impression.

First Impressions

Once you open the door, remember that your entrance hall, however big or small, will set the stage for your paying guests. Smell is a big factor in creating a welcoming atmosphere. Delicious aromas of baking bread, freshly brewed coffee or a fabulous scented candle wafting around the house will say 'Welcome – we are clean and inviting people.' Boiled cabbage or wet dog are definite turn-offs and will beg the question, if this is what the hall smells like, imagine the kitchen! They will notice the cobwebs, peeling paint and an overgrown garden with weeds even if you don't, so keep a watchful eye on maintenance and make sure the front of your house looks great at all times. If you do have a sign, make sure it looks fresh and welcoming. (Some signs will need planning permission so do contact the local planning office in your area with regard to signage.)

Fresh flowers are essential in a hall. A good doormat will be worth its weight in gold to protect floors, especially wooden ones. Keep umbrellas handy for guests arriving in downpours. Decor, of course, is up to you but dust, dirt, cobwebs and general untidiness are not acceptable. If your family members are in the habit of leaving bicycles and boots lying around, you will have to re-train them.

Smoking

Whether you allow smoking or not in your B&B is your choice. I would say that the majority of B&Bs do not allow smoking and it is becoming more and more difficult to smoke in public areas. If you are concerned about having smokers in your house, state clearly on all literature concerning your B&B (brochures, websites, cards, adverts, guides, etc.) that you do not allow smoking.

If you are a smoker, you need to be very careful and sensitive to guests who do not smoke. Non-smokers will not like staying in a bedroom that stinks of smoke.

Children and Pets

I group them together because, like smokers, you must decide if you want to take them. Put-up beds are a great way of accommodating children if you don't have family rooms. Going the route of travel cots and baby listening services is a matter of personal choice. Some B&Bs only take children over the age of 12. You must charge for children – the laundry costs are the same and they do eat breakfast, no matter what their parents say. In addition, beautiful rooms can occasionally be wrecked.

Pets fall into the same category as children (I write this as a mother and copious animal owner!). Dogs will invariably sleep on the bed so watch out for your bedspreads – it's a good idea to supply a blanket the owner can throw on top. I would make a standard charge for each pet and provide a space for them to run and do their ablutions if you decide to take them.

Locks

A lock on the door is crucial, as well as a bolt or chain for the guests' peace of mind. And have good locks installed on your own bedroom doors.

Give each guest a front door key and room key so that you are not waiting up for them until the wee small hours. It is a good idea to put them on a large, bulky key ring so that they won't forget about them or get them mixed up with their existing keys. Remember to collect the keys on checkout.

Good Housekeeping

Housekeeping is a matter of pride and organisation – it costs nothing to be clean, and clean you must be. Once you have sorted out your daily routine of stripping the beds, hoovering and dusting, it shouldn't take you more than 30 minutes to service a room. You should build in general dusting every day, including wiping over skirting boards, wardrobe tops and picture frames. I know I can service a room in 20 minutes if I'm pressed. Work to a timetable. The first couple of times you do it, naturally it will take you longer, but you will master the routine because it's your time you are wasting if you don't. If you want to make more money do all the work yourself, but if you can afford it, hire daily help.

Laundry

Laundry is the biggest challenge because even in a relatively small household, there is tons of it – so when you add guests' sheets and towels every day, it is a nightmare! It is cheapest to do it yourself. If not, either investigate a local laundry service or a linen hire company. It may cost you more but the stress of laundry will be gone.

The general rule of thumb is that you need a minimum of three sets of linen for each bed – two pillowcases, top sheet and bottom or flat sheet. One set should be on the bed, one set in the laundry and one set in the airing cupboard. The same goes for towels.

If you do your own laundry I advise you to use non-biological detergents as some people have allergies or sensitive skin. And invest in industrial-strength machines, especially quick dryers.

Bed Linen

Here's a guide to what you'll need for each guest.

Pillows

My husband always travels with his own pillows because he has been in the hotel business a long time. If pillows could talk they would tell you lots of stories. It is amazing what people get up to, so always use a pillow protector under the pillowcase and change it regularly. Allow two pillows per person.

Sheets

I have an aversion to polyester so it's Egyptian cotton or linen for me. John Lewis stores are brilliant for all your pillows, sheets, blankets and towels if you are going down your own laundry route. Their prices are usually very good unless you need vast quantities and can bulk-buy from a hotel supplier. The White Company also sells superb bed linen and has a very useful outlet shop in Bicester Village (see page 122).

Sheet Changes

We have a policy in our hotel that sheets are changed every night – the customer is paying full rate each night so in my opinion they should have clean sheets. I would say this applies to B&Bs as well unless you give a discount for stays of more than one night, but I can hear you all screaming about the laundry! So you may decide to change them every three nights for longer-staying customers. The choice is yours.

Blankets versus Duvets

This is a question of personal choice. I prefer sheets and a blanket but some people prefer a duvet. The workload is about the same. Some people who use duvets also put a sheet between it and the mattress so that you have a duvet cover, top sheet and bottom sheet, which is quite a lot of laundry, so I advise you to go the 'blanket, sheet' route. There is something rather nice about crawling into crisp, cold sheets. Whatever you decide, remember duvet covers must be changed just like sheets – a new one for each new guest.

Bedspreads

These are essential for finishing off the look of the room and I recommend quilted, patterned ones as they don't show the dirt as much as a solid-colour one. Please – no candlewick! Always have a couple of spare neutral ones to tone into the room design so that if there is an accident, you can quickly put a clean one on.

Throws

I like to see a throw neatly folded at the end of the bed so that guests don't have to destroy the bed if they are feeling a little chilly and can just spread it on top of them if they are napping or reading.

Furnishing the Bedroom

Obviously the rooms need to be fresh, clean and well maintained. The interior decor of the room is a matter of personal taste, but nothing looks worse than chipped paint and scruffy carpets.

Furniture doesn't have to match in terms of styles and periods, but all the pieces should blend well together and not look as though you went to the nearest junk shop and did a sweep! A chair, chest of drawers, bedside cabinets and hanging space is the minimum. If you have room, include a dressing table and stool which can also be used as a writing table.

If you don't have space for a wardrobe, fit a hanging rail or, at the very least, a few sturdy hooks. Provide good wooden hangers (don't be tempted to re-use hangers from the dry cleaners). A luggage rack is also useful.

The bed must be really comfortable, so choose a good mattress. In general, people never sleep very well away from home, so your B&B will score extra points if the bed is comfortable and your guests do sleep well. There should be a headboard, but try not to have a footboard as this can inconvenience tall guests. Mattress protectors are worth their weight in gold.

Lighting is very important – as well as good bedside lighting, an overhead light or lamp is needed. You could also provide a scented candle (with a suitable, stable holder), and don't forget the matches.

A full-length mirror, either on the back of a door or in a wardrobe, is a must. Make sure there is an electric socket near the mirror so guests can use the hairdryer.

Televisions are so cheap these days that you should try to put a large one in the room if proportions allow. Teletext is a must and Sky a bonus. Check that you can actually see the TV from the bed if you are lying down as this is how most people watch TV in a B&B.

Provide a metal waste bin. I don't know what people do but they always seem to fill the bin up. Waste bins can be a fire hazard, so metal is best.

Sleep in all the bedrooms yourself – be a guest in your own B&B. In this way, you (rather than your guests) will discover the niggles, such as a lamp in the wrong place or a noisy radiator.

Added Extras

Here's a checklist of extras that will transform your B&B into something special.

- Bathrobe
- Hot water bottle and cover
- Bottled water and a drinking glass
- Alarm clock
- Hairdryer (choose a compact yet powerful model)
- Radio
- DVD player plus a selection of CDs and DVDs
- Pack of playing cards
- Writing set (include paper, envelopes, postcards, stamps, pens, and a card with the address of your B&B)
- Books and up-to-date magazines (at the most, a few months old and change them if they become dog-eared)
- A small posy of flowers beside the bed – if they are from your garden, so much the better

- Sewing kit
- Information pack (containing local transport timetables, church services, information on places to eat and drink and the local sights)

The Dreaded Tea Tray!

Although I dislike tea trays in rooms, they are a must and you should provide them. All your wonderful ideas of serving your guests tea on arrival with home-made cakes and scones are a dream – the reality is that guests do not all come at the same time and it is a hassle. You will be up and down like a yo-yo and it will turn into a real pain, so you will need:

- 1 large tray
- 1 cup and saucer per person
- Sugar bowl
- Small biscuit tin, containing home-made biscuits of course!

- Canister(s) for tea (provide selection if you want) and good-quality instant coffee
- Teapot
- Teaspoons
- Milk jug – I recommend giving your guests fresh milk when they arrive (I hate those nasty little pots of UHT milk)
- Electric kettle

It is important to have a plug that is higher than usual so that the tea tray can sit on a table near the plug. You may want to consider installing a small, silent refrigerator so that you can leave fresh milk in the room, plus little foodie treats for your guests as well.

Bathrooms

The first thing you need to establish is whether it needs any building work – can you make an ensuite bathroom in the bedroom? Whatever you do, try not to destroy the character of the house – if it is a modern house, fitting in a bathroom might be straightforward, but I can't bear to see a beautiful big room with lovely cornices chopped off where a bathroom has been stuck in the corner. It isn't essential to have an ensuite bedroom (ensuite means a bedroom with a private bathroom integrated into the overall room) – a bedroom with its own private bathroom next door or across the corridor is fine, but ensuite is best.

The most important thing about a bathroom is that it is Clean! Clean! Clean! And nothing beats white and all its variations. I prefer white sanitaryware and tiles with perhaps a coloured relief, and I also recommend that the floor is easy to clean and not carpeted.

Powerful showers get lots of plus points and if you can't fit in a bath, put a shower in as big a space as you can.

Make sure you speak to your plumber about your hot water supply as you may well have nights and mornings when everyone will be bathing at the same time and there is nothing more irritating than running out of hot water.

Small bore electric lavatories are not a good idea and it is best to avoid them as sooner or later they will become a nightmare. If your plumbing is 'quaint', do put up a notice somewhere prominent to explain whether you are on mains drains or septic tanks, and how sanitary towels, etc. should be disposed of.

Good overhead lighting is a must and a smaller, lighted, magnified make-up mirror is very useful. Install a small table or shelf on which to put the contents of a sponge bag and if you have the room, a chair. Hooks on the back of the door are useful, and if possible add a heated towel rail. Do put in a shaving socket, and make sure there is a bin.

It's a good idea to provide small, individually wrapped bars of soap so that each guest can open a fresh bar.

The number of little touches you add to the bathroom will be up to you. Things like candles (remember the box of matches), cotton buds and pads, shampoo and conditioner, tampons and sanitary towels are always welcome. Be prepared to have them taken and replenish every day. Remember, you are running a business, not just having friends to stay who are forgiving.

Do NOT provide any drugs such as aspirin, as you may be held responsible if anything goes wrong.

Towels

Be generous. I always think people's spirit can be measured by the size of the towel they provide – there is nothing worse than being given small, worn towels. Make sure they have a good pile in them and absorb well. Each person will need a minimum of one hand towel and one bath sheet – and I do mean sheet – plus face cloth and bath mat. White works for me, but colour is up to you.

The Guest Sitting Room

If you have the space, it is a good idea to give your guests a sitting room and make it as comfortable as possible. What you want to avoid is having your own living space invaded.

It may be that you decide not to include a TV in the bedrooms, so you could have one available in the guest sitting room, for instance (make sure you have the right sort of TV licence – see page 126). The sitting room is a place where guests can meet others and usually people don't mind sharing. If you have a conservatory that doesn't get used much this would be perfect for the job. Try to make a couple of sitting areas according to how many bedrooms you let.

A selection of CDs or DVDs and videos for guest use and perhaps a board game and pack of playing cards along with a few books and magazines will make the space very welcoming. Of course, if the room has a fire or great view, make the most of it.

The Dining/Breakfast Room

The last impression when staying in a B&B is the breakfast, so every element of it must be wonderful, starting with the room you serve it in. If you have a dining room this is probably where you will serve breakfast. As with everywhere else in your B&B, it must be clean, neat and tidy. Ideally the room should be close to the kitchen and the decoration will reflect your personal choice. The great help with having a separate dining room is that you can set it the night before to spread the workload.

There are pros and cons about having one communal table and really it will be up to how you like to run your house. Some guests don't like to interact too much in the morning so separate tables would suit them better. One option, if the room is big enough, is to have a little table set as well as one large one. In my experience most people tend to sit at the communal table first.

A sideboard (all sorts of tables and pieces of furniture can be used) is a must as this is where you set out some of your delicious breakfast goodies for guests to serve themselves. Baskets of pastries, orange juice, cereals and other foods can be put onto the sideboard. Some people put a toaster out as well, for guests to make themselves hot toast.

Whatever you decide to do re seating arrangements, make sure that the tables don't wobble and the chairs are sturdy.

It is at this point that I just want to remind you that running a B&B will invade your personal space. Try to keep it to a minimum by being aware of guest rooms versus family rooms within the house, otherwise you will resent your paying guests and life will become very stressful. The financial rewards and friends made through the business are what keep most people going, and once you have a system up and running it will be easy.

Managing Bookings

Taking a booking
Overbooking
Registration
Checking in

With a mobile phone, you can take a booking wherever you are.

NOW THAT YOU have your permanent smile in place and the rooms are ready, you need to start taking bookings. The best way to control the bookings is to keep a diary.

If you are computer-friendly you may have a diary on your computer and can manage bookings by using a spreadsheet, but I recommend using a good old-fashioned paper diary. It will need to be large enough to fit in all the rooms on each date page. Divide each day into the number of rooms you have available. Clearly label each room on the date in the diary and the tariff should be accessible in case someone not familiar with the rooms or prices is taking the booking for you. Keep the diary by the main phone.

Remember to block off days that you won't be taking bookings for and highlight days that events in your area are taking place so that you can be ready for the onslaught.

It may be that you will have a minimum stay for such events (e.g. the booking for a weekend must be a minimum of two nights or a special event is three nights only). This will help you to maximise your occupancy levels and ensure you don't miss out on bookings during peak times.

With the advent of the mobile phone you can now take a booking wherever you are so long as you have the diary with you. It is a good idea to learn how to divert your main booking landline to your mobile or vice versa. Don't forget to switch it back when you are home.

Taking a Booking

You will need enough space in your diary to write down all the relevant questions such as:

* Name
* Address and telephone number
* Number of guests
* Date of booking
* Duration of the stay
* Special requirements
* Method of payment
* How they heard about you (essential to see whether your marketing is working)

Ask for a deposit and a letter or email of confirmation. If you accept credit cards you can take down the number and treat it as a deposit.

So your diary might look something like this:

Friday 3rd June 2005

Blue Room dbl £35.00 per person
Mr and Mrs Joe Smith – 2 guests, 2 nights
7 Acacia Ave, Any town, Any county, UK AB12 CD3
01234 567890
Date of booking 03/05/05
Allergic to wheat
Will send cheque for first night as deposit
Alastair Sawday guide

If the deposit and letter of confirmation don't arrive within 3–4 days, ring to see what is happening. Nothing should be confirmed without a deposit. It will happen – you will wait for someone who didn't send anything and you will miss out on a booking and, yes, it will probably be during your busiest week or weekend. Don't beat yourself up about it but learn from your mistakes: always take a deposit to consider the booking safe.

The Two-Night Booking

This is purely up to you but there are times when taking a booking for two nights is a much better option. If you have a seasonal business and weekends are always full, you may want to take bookings for only two nights so you will never have an empty room on one or other night. If there are special events such as a concert or sporting event taking place it is a good idea only to take bookings for two nights. Most people do this as it is less hassle and more profitable.

It is a good idea to have a cancellation policy and be prompt with refunds if applicable.

Overbooking

This will happen at some point too! You will have taken two bookings for the same room on the same night. Don't panic! Brace yourself because the customer will be livid. Keep calm and call to get them a booking at the nearest decent B&B – if it is more expensive than yours, maybe agree to pay the difference. Most people will not let you pay and be understanding, but there are always a few. If you can't find anywhere nearby, keep going until you do, and smile throughout and apologise.

If the scene turns nasty and you have done all you can to sort out the situation, remember it is still your house and you don't have to have them even if you did have a room, so feel free to turf them out.

Registration

I suggest you invest in a good-quality bound book that is divided into columns such as date, name, address, passport details, and room name/number. Ask the guests to 'check in' and sign the book.

You can also use a guest registration card with the same details on it. For foreign guests you will need their passport numbers. Guests' details must be kept for a minimum of 12 months. The registration must be available for inspection by the police or other authorised bodies at all times.

You will need a register of who should be in the building, at what time, in case a roll-call is needed in the event of a fire.

There is a legal requirement to hold information on guests over the age of 16. The Data Protection Act will soon kick into place so do get a copy to know how it affects you and your business. See page 126 for details.

Checking In

The welcome and the departure are the most critical times for impressing your guests. When guests arrive they are nearly always stressed! One or the other will probably have got the map-reading wrong, resulting in an argument in the car, the children will be going nuts in the back or the dog hasn't travelled as well as it could have done. So it is up to you to make sure they are cosseted and calmed down.

Good directions to your B&B are essential. Include rail travel options, car directions from north, south, east, west or directions from airports or railway stations. Maps are very useful and can be e-mailed, faxed or sent ahead of time. In town locations you will want to give clear directions about parking, where to etc. In an ideal world, if parking is very difficult, you can take out valet parking insurance and offer to park your guest's car! If this a step too far for you, have the exact coins needed for meters or pay-and-display machines in little envelopes with enough change (you can add it on to the bill) for 24 hours inside so that when the guest arrives and asks about parking you are ready for them and immediately relieve the stress of finding small change.

Check-in is the time to ask about newspapers and wake-up calls if you provide them. Guests may ask about dining in the area and restaurant recommendations.

Always offer to take up luggage and when you take them up to their room show them where lights, bathroom and welcome packs are, and how things like the TV/satellite/ radio work. If you provide tea trays in the rooms, take the fresh milk up as soon as you see them to the room. Otherwise offer them tea on arrival and bring it up promptly as most people are desperate for a cuppa.

Breakfast

The kitchen
Setting the table
Serving breakfast
How to cook a full breakfast
Eggs

6

A delicious breakfast is as important as a comfortable bed.

SERVING YOUR GUESTS a delicious breakfast is just as important as providing them with a comfortable room to sleep in. The breakfast will provide their final memory of your B&B, so make sure it is a good one.

If you decide to cater for special dietary requirements, I suggest you ask the relevant questions at the time of taking the booking so that you will be prepared.

The Kitchen

First and foremost, your kitchen will now be serving food for the general paying public. I strongly recommend that you contact your local Environmental Health Officer to provide answers to all of your questions concerning food safety (see page 25). As in the other areas we have already covered, cleanliness is paramount. You do not want to run the risk of food poisoning. I recommend that you attend a Health and Hygiene Food Safety course for food handlers. The majority of food poisoning still occurs mainly in domestic kitchens and that is exactly what you will be working in.

You need to practise due diligence when serving and cooking food. You are responsible for sourcing foods from reputable food suppliers who also practise due diligence. For instance, buy salmonella-free eggs from a supplier you know and trust. I'm the first one to say support your local farmers' markets, farmers and shops, but you will need to be assured by all your suppliers that all the ingredients they are supplying to you are of the highest standards and meeting all the legislation required.

The layout of any kitchen should always have fluidity and convenience in mind. A good refrigerator and freezer will come into their own. Plenty of workspace, a good dishwasher and washing-up area will be an enormous help. You must be comfortable with the cooker you are using and if you are lucky enough to have an Aga, hooray – breakfast will be a doddle! Check your electrical appliances regularly for safety and temperatures, making sure they comply with mandatory regulations.

Commercial-grade washing detergents should be used as many domestic dishwashing machines do not reach over 60°C.

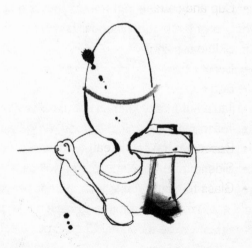

Setting the Table

Crockery and cutlery will be of personal design choice. Stainless steel is easier to keep polished and looking good than silver, and a china service that is widely available will mean that breakages can be quickly rectified.

For each place setting you will need:

- Cup and saucer
- Dinner plate
- Side plate
- Cereal bowl
- Egg cup
- Table knife and fork
- Teaspoon
- Dessertspoon for cereal
- Side knife
- Glass for juice
- Napkin

Couples can share teapots, hot-water jugs, coffee pots, toast racks, milk jugs and sugar basins; otherwise have enough of everything else for each guest. I like toast served in toast racks as that way it doesn't become soggy.

A word about napkins: of course, linen is best, but in reality good-quality paper ones are preferable due to laundry loads. You can ring the changes with different coloured paper napkins. If you choose linen, you can always ask the laundry service (if you use one) to launder them.

Serving Breakfast

Breakfast is one of the hardest meals to get absolutely right – everything must be cooked to order and is usually for large numbers of people. Toast, eggs, bacon, etc. can all become a nightmare. The answer is to keep it simple and never, never try out a new recipe on paying guests! Sourcing really good-quality foods will give you a major head start – if the ingredients are good you are more than halfway to a great breakfast. I prefer to cook and eat seasonally, so you may want to bear this in mind when you are planning your menus.

I suggest that your menu should look something like this:

Full breakfast
(eggs, bacon, sausage, tomato, fried bread and mushrooms)
Kippers
Selection of cereals and yoghurts
Freshly squeezed orange juice
Home-made jams and marmalade
Basket of pastries, croissants and muffins
Hot toast
Tea or coffee

Most people will have a variation of the full cooked breakfast – some may want poached, scrambled or boiled eggs rather than fried (see pages 91–93).

Kippers

Kippers are usually welcomed by male guests as they hardly ever get them at home because of the smell. I think the best ones are Craster kippers from L. Robson & Sons in Northumberland (tel. 01665 576223).

To cook kippers, put them on a shallow baking tray lined with Bake-O-Glide, splash on a bit of water and a knob of butter and cook them under a really hot grill for about 5–8 minutes. If using an Aga, cook them in the Roasting Oven for 8–10 minutes. Alternatively, put them into a deep stoneware jug (tail up) and pour over boiling water to cover. Leave to stand for 8–10 minutes, then drain. Serve with plenty of butter and hot toast.

Tea and Coffee

Coffee and tea must be freshly made for each guest. Nothing is worse than coffee-makers that are switched on at the crack of dawn so the coffee is disgusting by the time the first guest comes down. If you can go the whole hog, invest in an electric bean-to-cup coffee machine – Gaggia do a very good one. If not, go for a coffee percolator – I know it sounds old-fashioned but they do make great coffee. Remember that some people prefer decaffeinated coffee.

Loose leaf tea will be very welcome to the tea drinkers and you may want to offer Earl Grey as well a good English Breakfast blend. You can buy teapots with metal strainers already in them (see page 123) which are very easy to use (nylon strainers tend to break). Make sure you also serve hot water with the tea.

Rather than making your own croissants, I recommend buying frozen French croissant dough. Thaw it overnight and bake the croissants in the morning, so that you can serve them straight out of the oven.

Waiting at Table

The rules about serving are put down on the left and remove from the right. Have things like sugar, salt and pepper on the table as well as a small, neat flower arrangement. Keep pets out of the dining room. The person serving breakfast should be clean, neat and tidy, hair tied back and jewellery kept to a minimum. Avoid wearing strong scent.

Have a sideboard in the dining room and lay out the juice and cereals for people to help themselves.

When guests arrive in the dining room, take their order and direct them to help themselves to cereal and juice.

How to Cook a Full Breakfast

This is what you should generally allow per person:

- 1 or 2 fried eggs
- 2 rashers of bacon (back or streaky)
- 1 sausage
- 1 large field mushroom
- Half a tomato
- Fried bread

Conventional Method

1. First cook the sausages. Pre-heat the oven to 200°C/400°F/gas 6. I recommend using Bake-O-Glide (see page 124) as not only does it stop foods from sticking but helps with the washing up too! Line a shallow baking tray with Bake-O-Glide and place the sausages on top. Do not prick them! Drizzle over a little sunflower oil and put them into the pre-heated oven.

Cook for 20–25 minutes or until browned and cooked in the middle. Turn them halfway through cooking time. When they are ready, keep warm in a warmed ovenproof dish. You can also cook them in a pre-heated frying pan with some oil in it – I suggest you invest in a splash guard (a wire mesh cover that prevents the fat from spitting all over you).

2. While the sausages are cooking, cut the tomatoes in half. Place them in an ovenproof dish with the mushrooms and drizzle over some more oil. Season with salt and pepper and slide them into the oven as well – they will take about 15 minutes. If the tomatoes are small, watch them as they may collapse in a heap! Keep warm when they are done.

3. If you are using a frying pan for the sausages you may also like to use it for cooking the bacon, although you can also grill it. Drain off any hot fat to a suitable container and wipe out the inside of the pan with kitchen

paper. Add more clean sunflower oil. Heat up over a medium heat and fry the bacon until crispy or however you like to serve it. Remove it and drain on kitchen paper.

4. Turn up the heat and fry the slice of bread – the fat does need to be hot for this. Remove and drain next to bacon. Keep warm.

5. When you are ready to cook the eggs, assemble the sausage, bacon, tomato, mushroom and fried bread on the plate and keep warm.

6. Eggs must be fried in clean fat. Heat up about 150ml clean sunflower oil in a large, wide, seasoned frying pan. It is essential to use fresh eggs when frying as otherwise the whites will spread around the pan and they will be hard to get out. Eggs must go into hot fat otherwise they will absorb too much fat and taste greasy. If you are confident the eggs are fresh, crack them straight into the hot fat; if not, crack them onto a saucer and slide them

into the pan. Do not overcrowd the pan and add too many eggs – two at a time is best. Baste the eggs with some of the hot fat to seal the top. When ready, remove them with a large fish slice, drain the bottom on kitchen towel and place on the plate. Serve straight away.

You must serve breakfast on warm or hot plates. It's very useful to have a separate warming plate or cabinet to heat plates and keep food warm.

Aga Method

1. Depending on how many you are cooking for, use either the half-size Aga roasting tin or the full-size one. Line it with Bake-O-Glide, and put the mushrooms and tomato halves, cut side up, on the bottom of the tin. Drizzle over a little oil and season with salt and pepper. Place the grill rack on top and put the sausages on the rack over the mushrooms and tomatoes (do not prick the sausages). Slide the tin on to the first (highest) set of runners in the Roasting Oven, and cook for 10 minutes.

2. When the timer goes off, take the tin out of the oven, turn the sausages and lay the bacon rashers on the grill rack. Pop it back into the Roasting Oven for a further 10 minutes. Depending on the thickness of the bacon and the size of the sausages, you may need to adjust the timings slightly.

3. When everything is cooked, take the tin of the oven and put the bacon, sausage, tomato and mushroom on a warmed platter. Cover with foil and transfer to the Simmering Oven to keep warm while you cook the eggs. (If you want well-done bacon, after you transfer the sausages, tomatoes and mushrooms to the platter, take off the grill rack and put the bacon on the bottom of the tin. Place the tin on the floor of the Roasting Oven and let the bacon cook to your liking.)

4. To make fried bread, do it in exactly the same way as above for well-done bacon, adding more oil if necessary. It will probably take about 5 minutes each side.

5. There are two ways of cooking fried eggs, in the Aga and on the Aga (see next page).

Method 1 - in the Aga

Use the same tin that the bacon, etc. is cooked in. When you remove the sausages, tomatoes, etc., add a little more oil to the tin and put it onto the Roasting Oven floor to get really hot. When the oil is hot, crack the eggs into the tin one at a time. The large tin will take about 6 large eggs and the half-size tin about 3 large eggs. Baste the eggs with the fat and put the tin back into the oven for approximately 3 minutes or until they are done to your liking.

Method 2 - on the Aga

Open the Simmering Plate lid and either grease it with a little oil, or use a round pre-cut circle of Bake-O-Glide (I always use this) and put it directly onto the Simmering Plate surface. Drizzle a little oil onto kitchen paper and rub it over the plate. Crack the egg onto the hot surface and close the lid. The egg will cook in about 2 minutes. The Simmering Plate surface can take about 3 large eggs at a time. (If you have an older Aga and the lid is dented, check to see if it touches the top of the egg when you close the lid. If it does, leave the lid open. The egg will take a little longer to cook.)

6. To make toast, use the Aga toasting rack (the thing that looks like a tennis racket). Open the rack, put sliced bread in and place on the Boiling Plate. Close the lid but keep an eye on it as it will toast very quickly, then turn over to do the other side. To stop very fresh bread from sticking to the toaster, heat the rack up first on the Boiling Plate before putting in the toast. If you like crispy toast, leave the Boiling Plate lid open.

Eggs

Although fried eggs usually accompany a full breakfast, guests will sometimes request scrambled, poached or boiled.

Scrambled Eggs

Crack two eggs per person into a glass bowl. Add a little salt, white pepper and 1–2 tbsp double cream and beat the eggs gently. Melt the butter in a non-stick saucepan over a medium heat (or on the Simmering Plate of an Aga) and pour in the eggs. Stir constantly with a wooden fork or spoon until the eggs just start to form soft curds. Remove from the heat and stir until it is cooked to the required consistency.

Poached Eggs

I don't believe in egg poachers! All you need is a large frying pan with clean water. You do need very fresh eggs for poaching. If the eggs are stale, they will spread like mad and be a disaster.

This is a foolproof method for poaching eggs. Bring a wide frying pan with enough water to cover the eggs up to a gentle simmer over a medium heat (or on the Simmering

Plate of an Aga). As soon as you see the first bubbles start to appear, crack the eggs into the pan and set a timer for 1 minute. After 1 minute, remove the pan from the heat and re-set the timer for 10 minutes. When cooked, remove the eggs from the water with a slotted spoon, drain on a piece of kitchen paper and serve straight away. Alternatively, crack the eggs into gently simmering water and cook for 2–3 minutes.

Boiled Eggs

Ask your guest how they want their boiled eggs. This is the method for a 4-minute egg which will give you a cooked white but soft yolk: just right for dipping in your soldiers! An accurate kitchen timer is essential.

Bring a small saucepan of water up to the boil, then turn the heat down to a gentle simmer (or move the pan to the Simmering Plate) and lower the eggs in one at a time. Set the timer for 4 minutes. Remove with a slotted spoon and serve with hot buttered toast soldiers.

Always use fresh organic eggs. Store eggs in a cool place in either an egg rack or in their own box. Eggshells are porous and will pick up other smells so always keep them in a well-ventilated area away from strong-smelling foods.

Knowing Your Market

Creating good PR
Marketing your B&B
B&B guidebooks

Good PR starts with the smile on your face as you open the door.

MARKETING AND PR are two different things, but this is your business, so you will have to be good at both. In a nutshell, marketing concerns paying for adverts and guide entries and PR concerns selling your product (that's you and your B&B) to journalists and others who can recommend and write about you without paying for it.

Creating Good PR

Good PR will start with the smile on your face as you open the door and end with the smile on your face as the guest leaves. PR involves wooing people to get them on your side so that they recommend your B&B above anyone else's. So, for instance, make an appointment with your local tourist board and tell them about yourself and your product. Take them brochures and invite them to have a look around your establishment so they can see for themselves how great it is.

One of the first places that a journalist goes to is the local tourist board when they are writing about an area. You may be asked to put up journalists free of charge and I suggest that you do if possible, as it could lead to a mention in the piece they are writing – but be discerning and upfront about what is in it for you.

Marketing Your B&B

Marketing is more about choosing the guides that can get you the most business and you will probably be paying for the service. So do your research.

Identify your market. If you live in the centre of a town or city you will want to attract business from local companies and this will give you your bread-and-butter trade, which will more than likely be Monday to Friday, four nights a week. Find out how the company makes accommodation bookings and use the system – some like to do it through travel agents so see if you can get on their books; others ask the MD's PA to do it, so get to know her and take her out for lunch once in a while. There is absolutely no point in going into a guide that deals mainly with B&Bs in the country. However, you may have a particularly good theatre, opera house or sports stadium nearby and you may want to be included in their brochures so that you can pick up weekend business.

If your B&B is in the country, capitalise on the beauty of your area and local attractions. Tourist boards are a good place to start because they stock the brochures for all your local attractions and events. Look at guides that attract customers who are interested in walking, heritage, gardens or whatever the USP (unique selling point) is for your area. If you have a country house hotel nearby, it is very likely that they will have times when the hotel is full and could pass on trade – weddings are a typical example. Go to see the manager and invite them to come and have a look so that they are confident when recommending your B&B to their guests. Look at the fixtures list for events in your area so that you know when you will be inundated with calls and bookings.

If you live near a pretty church, chances are that a lot of people will want to use it for weddings, so get to know the local vicar. Invite him round for tea and give him some of your cards to hand out to future brides.

Create Your Own Website

Do set up your own website, or hire a web company to do it. It doesn't have to be very complicated. Keep it looking fresh and easy to use. Include basic information about location, tariff, a photograph of the outside and a few rooms. It is great to have a map and directions on how to get to you as most people have internet access and can print it off. Of course you can also have your email as part of it.

Try and set up reciprocal links from tourist board websites and local tourist attractions. Make sure you are also listed on all the relevant search engines – your web company will know how to do this.

Brochures

Your brochure can either mirror the design of your website or you can just have a good-quality postcard with all your details, guiding people to your website for further information. I think pictures say more than words and that is what people are really interested in so if you do invest a lot in a brochure, try to include as many photographs as possible.

Business cards are also useful as you can pass them out to all and sundry.

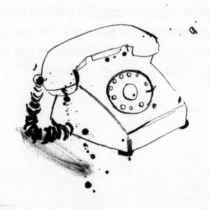

B&B Guidebooks

There are many B&B guidebooks on the market, and the best ones are regularly updated. Have a good look through the various guides in your local bookshop or online before deciding which one you would like to be featured in. I am a huge fan of the Michelin guide but for some people the information is too brief, so looking through the AA Bed and Breakfast Guide is a good start. Alastair Sawday does a very nice B&B guide. There are even specialist B&B guides for garden lovers and dog-owners!

Once you have decided which guide you'd like to be in, phone other B&Bs already in the guide and ask whether they're happy with the trade they are getting from it. See pages 124–5 for further advice.

Guidebook Inspections

When inspectors from associations inspect a B&B they have certain criteria that the establishment must fulfil in order to be awarded points that will give the overall mark for classification for the guide. The AA do a very good job at setting these guidelines and it is good practice to contact them for an AA Quality Standards guide for AA-recognised guest accommodation.

What the guidelines can never be exact about is how you interpret them, so having a chair in the room for one person might mean a bog-standard comfortable chair and for another it could mean a beautifully upholstered chair with goose-down cushions. All this is down to personal taste and budget.

Money Matters

Making out bills
VAT + income tax
B+B costings
Setting your tariff

Estimating the cost of everything
is essential, right down to the cost
of each teabag.

I STRONGLY ADVISE you to have a chat with a qualified chartered accountant to find out what will be expected of you regarding bank accounts, VAT and income tax. All figures given in this chapter should be treated as guidelines only and were correct at the time of going to press.

Making Out Bills

Keep payment easy and try to set your tariff in round
numbers – it makes life a lot simpler.

Present your guests with a bill on check-out. Remember
to deduct the deposit paid. The method of payment is up to
you and if you feel it is necessary to take credit cards your
bank will be only too happy to set it up for you. If you take a
cheque, make sure it is filled in correctly and write down the
cheque guarantee card details on the back. You will need a
certain amount of cash for change and I suggest you invest
in a safe.

A typical bill may look like this:

Mr and Mrs Joe Smith
1 night's stay in a double room   *£50.00*
Date of stay
Deposit paid   *£10.00*

Total   *£40.00*

Today's date

You may also want to do this in a receipt book or on
headed paper. I suggest giving the guest the top copy of the
bill and keeping the duplicate for yourself.

VAT and Income Tax

I strongly suggest you seek a qualified accountant, one with
accommodation-provider experience, to answer these
questions and bring to light any other queries that may arise.
Ask about the VAT threshold and whether you are liable.

The questions listed here are only some of the ones that should be asked. When it comes to tax, ignorance is not a defence!

I hate to bring this up, but you should be aware of what the Inland Revenue may demand from you at one time or another. Certain things can affect which taxes are due and when, such as:

- how many months of the year you are open
- the percentage of your house that is given over to B&B
- whether you are rated as a business
- capital gains tax when you sell
- repairs and renewals – what percentage you can claim for

If your property is mortgaged, you may need permission from your mortgage lender to run your home as a business, so do talk to them.

B&B Costings

Estimating the cost of everything is essential. The basic items that you need to look at and, of course, the cost of the items will vary due to location and quality.

Food Costs

Work out costs per person. To do this take the unit price of the item; say, for instance, it costs £2.04 for a packet of organic mushrooms and there are 6 in the pack, it would be 204 divided by 6 which equals £0.34 per mushroom per person. If you buy items by weight you will have to count the average slices (say, bacon) and weigh one slice and work it out.

I worked out (at the time of going to press) that the full cooked breakfast of 2 eggs, 2 rashers bacon, sausage, tomato, mushroom and fried bread cost £2.89 per person. All in – if they had everything from cereal to kippers – it would cost £4.98 per person You only need to do this arithmetic every so often because once you have a base price you can go up from there. Things like cereals sometimes tell you how many portions are in the pack so you can work out an average cost. Other items you may have to 'guestimate', such as coffee and tea per pot or bag. The basic rule of thumb for a cup of tea or coffee is about 15p. You may want to consider providing little pre-portioned individual boxes of cereal to avoid waste.

Food costs must not be more than 35% of overall food sales.

Other Sundry Costs

Loo roll and tissues can be guestimated as well – you can't
very well go about counting every sheet and estimating
individual usage! Say a box of tissues costs £1.55 and it
lasts 7 days, so the cost is £0.22 per person per day. Half a
roll of loo paper is about £0.30. Toiletries are expensive but
I guestimate £2.00 per person or more.

Please do not economise on loo roll! It is so silly to put
beautiful linen on the beds and flowers in the room, and
then have nasty lavatory paper!

Laundry costs can be worked out as above if you are
doing your own – don't forget to include utilities when doing
so. If you use a hire company or laundry service they will
have a piece price. The average price for laundry per person
per night (including napkin, tablecloth (half per person),

2 sheets, 2 pillowcases, 2 towels, bath mat) is £3.85.
If using duvets rather than blankets, add the cost of
laundering the covers. Also, remember that bedspreads
need laundering too. The benefit of using a hire company
is that you don't have any cost of purchase of linen or
deprecation of linen.

Budgets will have to be set for things like PR, guide
inclusion, advertising costs, brochures and stationery (see
page 97–103).

Setting Your Tariff

After working out the costs, you must decide what the
market can stand, what you are prepared to work for, and
whether it is worth your while doing B&B. In my experience
B&Bs make good money but you must look at this carefully.

I think that today it may cost you in the region of £10.00
per person per night considering all the costs listed above.
You must know what your costs are to work out whether it

is worthwhile doing B&B. The tariff you set and charge will be down to market force, supply and demand. If you know that the average B&B in your area is charging £22.00 per person per night and offering identical services then that will be a consideration – but you must consider like for like. It's no good comparing them with you if you are offering linen sheets and organic foods and they are using polyester sheets and the cheapest food money can buy. Also bear in mind that it is very hard to go up in price in leaps and bounds – it is better to set a higher price as it is never good business to drop your prices unless you have built in a discount system.

Items To Be Costed

Breakfast:

- Full cooked breakfast (bacon, 2 eggs, sausage, tomato, mushroom and fried bread)
- Kippers
- Fruit juice

- Tea/coffee
- Milk
- Sugar
- Toast
- Butter
- Jam/marmalade
- Pastries
- Yoghurts
- Cereals
- Sauces
- Napkin
- Tablecloth
- Wastage
- Breakages

Room:
- Tea tray in room (coffee, tea, milk, sugar, biscuits)
- Bottled water
- Newspaper
- Loo roll

- Tissues
- Toiletries (soap, shampoo, conditioner, body lotion)
- Laundry (2 sheets, 2 pillowcases, bath sheet, small towel, face cloth, bathmat)
- Flowers
- Breakages

Overheads:
- Utilities
- Theft
- Breakages
- Wear and tear
- Staff
- Telephone
- Stationery
- Postage
- PR
- Bank charges for credit cards

Useful Addresses

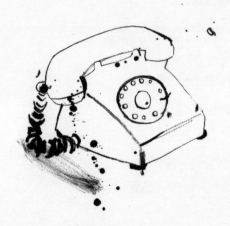

Here are a few useful contacts from my address book.

Amy Willcock
www.amywillcock.co.uk

The George Hotel
Quay Street
Yarmouth
Isle of Wight PO41 0PE
01983 760331
www.thegeorge.co.uk

Rangeware
(Amy's range of cookware)
Mermaid
0121 554 2001
www.mermaidcookware.com

Chic Kit
(Amy's range of kitchen textiles)
ICTC
01603 488019
www.ictc.co.uk

Raynaudes
Orlando Murrin's B&B in France
www.raynaudes.com

Bed Suppliers

Sleepeezee
020 8540 9171
www.sleepeezee.co.uk

Bed Linen

Combined Linen Services (CLS)
01626 882992
www.cls-group.co.uk

John Lewis
Head office 020 7828 1000
www.johnlewis.com

The White Company
0870 900 9555
www.thewhitecompany.com
also at Bicester Outlet Village
01869 323200
www.bicestervillage.co.uk

General Supplies
(china, cutlery, toiletries, stationery)

ICTC
01603 488019
www.ictc.co.uk

Arthur Price of England
01543 257775
www.arthurprice.com
(suppliers of Guy Degrenne teapots with in-built strainers)

Guest International
01189 817377
www.guestint.co.uk

Aslotel Ltd
01372 362533
www.aslotel.co.uk

Floris
mail order 0845 702 3239
www.florislondon.com

Tottering By Gently
01959 569301
www.tottering.com
(great lavatory signs)

Swantex Paper Products
0870 777 7926
www.swantex.com

Aga Rayburn
01952 642000
www.aga-rayburn.co.uk

Bake-O-Glide
01706 224 790
www.bakeoglide.co.uk

Viking Direct Stationery
0800 845464
www.viking-direct.co.uk

Guides

AA Hotel Services
01256 844455
www.theAA.com

Wolsey Lodges
01473 822058
www.wolsey-lodges.co.uk

The Pink Booklet
Visit Britain
0208 846 9000
www.visitbritain.com

B&B UK
www.bed-and-breakfast.org

Bed & Breakfast Nationwide
01255 831235
www.bedandbreakfastnationwide.com

Michelin
01923 205247
www.michelin.co.uk

Alistair Sawday
01275 464891
www.sawdays.co.uk

Legal Matters

Custom and Excise
0845 010 9000
www.hmce.gov.uk

Inland Revenue
0845 9000404
www.inlandrevenue.gov.uk

Data Protection
01625 545740
www.dataprotection.gov.uk

TV Licensing
08705 763763
www.tvlicensing.co.uk

Tourist Boards

There nine regional tourist boards throughout England, plus separate ones for Wales and Scotland. My best advice is to contact Visit Britain (see page 125) to find out the details for your area.

Organic Food and Farmers' Markets

The Soil Association
0117 929 0661
www.soilassociation.org

National Association of Farmers' Markets
0845 230 2150
www.farmersmarkets.net

Cookery Schools

Amy Willcock
www.amywillcock.co.uk
01983 760331
I run cookery workshops which include Aga Know-How
courses, B&B Know-How and Lifestyle.

Eggleston Hall
01833 650 553
www.egglestonhall.co.uk

Leith's School of Food and Wine
0207 229 0177
www.leiths.com

Lyn Hall
La Petite Cuisine
0207 584 6841

Author's Acknowledgements

Huge thanks to everyone who has helped with this book:
Warren Haynes at the Isle of Wight Environmental Health
Department; Neil Gunn, Chairman of Wolsey Lodges;
Derek Bulmer, Editor of Michelin Guide; Sue McGeaoch,
The Grange B&B; and my parents, Iris and Bart Zuzik.
My books are always a team effort and special thanks to
my editor Gillian Haslam, my agent Sarah Wooldridge,
and my husband Jeremy.

Index